FIRST ROUTINES

EATING HEALTHY FOODS

by Jenna Lee Gleisner

I0801083

TABLE OF CONTENTS

tadpole books

WORDS TO KNOW

apples

carrots

cheese

eggs

healthy foods

oatmeal

EATING HEALTHY FOODS

Let's eat healthy foods!

apple

I eat apples.

I eat eggs.

cheese

I eat cheese.

carrot

I eat carrots.

oatmeal

I eat oatmeal.

What foods do you eat?

LET'S REVIEW!

There are five main food groups. They are fruits, vegetables, grains, protein, and dairy. Which groups do these foods belong to?

INDEX